Susan Rivers • Setsuko Toyama

English Time 1

Student Book

2nd Edition

OXFORD
UNIVERSITY PRESS

OXFORD
UNIVERSITY PRESS

Great Clarendon Street, Oxford, OX2 6DP, United Kingdom

Oxford University Press is a department of the University of Oxford.
It furthers the University's objective of excellence in research, scholarship,
and education by publishing worldwide. Oxford is a registered trade
mark of Oxford University Press in the UK and in certain other countries

ISBN 978 0 19 400502 9 STUDENT BOOK
ISBN 978 0 19 400500 5 STUDENT CD
ISBN 978 0 19 400506 7 STUDENT PACK

Printed in China

This book is printed on paper from certified and well-managed sources

ACKNOWLEDGEMENTS

*The Publishers would like to thank the following for their kind permission to reproduce
photographs:* Alamy pp.47 (© Nigel Cattlin/field of potatoes), 73 (© Nigel Cattlin/
field of potatoes); BananaStock p.32 (boy in blue); iStockphoto pp.15 (BruceBlock/
spider, Mac99/fly, ElementalImaging/bee), 16 (JBryson/girl in white),
31 (gjohnstonphoto/pencils), 70 (ElementalImaging/bee), 71 (Mac99/fly),
73 (BruceBlock/spider); Photodisc pp.32 (girl), 48 (girl with hair band);
Photolibrary.com pp.47 (Peter Arnold Images/Dan Porges/orange grove, Ticket/
Margaret Walton/cows), 70 (Ticket/Margaret Walton/cows), 72 (Peter Arnold
Images/Dan Porges/orange grove); Shutterstock pp.15 (Cathy Keifer/caterpillar),
31 (ekler/ruler), 32 (Gelpi/pencil sharpeners), 47 (huyangshu/rice paddy), 70 (Cathy
Keifer/caterpillar), 72 (huyangshu/rice paddy), 73 (huyangshu/rice paddy).

Commissioned photography by: Graham Alder p.32 (boy in red); Gareth Boden
pp.16 (girl in pink), 48 (girl in pink), 64 (girl in pink, boy); Mark Mason pp.16,
48, 64 (boy in red).

Main illustrations by: Tyson Smith/Anna Goodson Management

Other illustrations by: Gabriele Antonini/Advocate-Art (Digger's World); Kathy
Baxendale pp.48 (food collage), 64; Beccy Blake (worms); Steve Cox Illustrations
(Songs and Chants); Rachel Fuller pp.16, 32, 48 (survey); Sophie Rohrbach/The
Organisation (Phonics Time); Mark Ruffle pp.31, 63, 70 (tree), 72 (tree, maths),
73 (tree roots, seed), 74 (tree branch).

Cover illustration by: Paul Gibbs

Musical arrangements and chant music by: William Hirtz

Original characters developed by: Amy Wummer

Acknowledgement:

I thank Lesley Koustaff for her insight, guidance, and endurance.
I thank Shoko Noguchi, Eiko Tsuchida, and Mieko Masuo for their
support and encouragement.
I thank OUP for making this series a reality.

Setsuko Toyama

Table of Contents

Syllabus

Unit	Unit title	Topic	Conversation Time	Word Time	Practice Time	Phonics Time
1	In the Neighborhood	People and animals	Good morning. Hello! How are you? Fine, thank you.	Annie Ted Digger girl boy dog	I'm Annie. I'm a girl. You're Ted. You're a boy.	Bb ball bird boy Pp pencil point pizza
2	In the Meadow	Nature	Ah-choo! Bless you! Thanks.	tree butterfly flower cloud bird lake	This is a butterfly. That's a bird.	Gg garden girl gorilla Kk kangaroo key kite
3	On the Farm	Farm animals	Sh! Be quiet! Sorry. That's okay.	goat cow horse chicken sheep cat	What's this? It's a goat. What's that? It's a cow.	Mm milk mop mother Nn net night nurse

Review of Units 1–3

Cross-curricular 1: Nature   bee   caterpillar   fly   spider
Project Time: Bugs Poster

Unit	Unit title	Topic	Conversation Time	Word Time	Practice Time	Phonics Time
4	At the Stationery Store	School supplies	Here you are. Thanks. You're welcome.	pen book eraser pencil ruler pencil case	Is it a pen? Yes, it is. Is it an eraser? No, it isn't. It's a pencil.	Dd desk dog duck Tt table teacher tiger
5	At School	Numbers	What's your first name? Emily. What's your last name? Young.	one (1) seven (7) two (2) eight (8) three (3) nine (9) four (4) ten (10) five (5) eleven (11) six (6) twelve (12)	How many cows? One cow. Two cows.	Hh hand horse house Ww water window woman
6	In Gym Class	Feelings	Ouch! Are you okay? I think so.	happy sad cold hot hungry thirsty	Are you happy? Yes, I am. No, I'm not. I'm sad.	Ff feet fish fork Vv van vase violin

Review of Units 4–6

Cross-curricular 2: Math Problems   math problem   plus   equals   minus
Project Time: Math Problems Poster

Unit	Unit title	Topic	Conversation Time	Word Time	Practice Time	Phonics Time
7	At the Food Court	Food	Are you finished? No, not yet. Please hurry!	burgers salad rice fish spaghetti pizza	I/You like burgers. I/You don't like pizza.	Ss sea sock soup Zz zebra zipper zoo
8	At the Supermarket	Fruits and vegetables	May I borrow a pen? Sure. Here you are. Thanks.	apples oranges bananas cucumbers potatoes carrots	Do you like apples? Yes, I do. No, I don't.	short a ant bag hat map
9	At the Circus	Physical descriptions	What's wrong? I feel sick. That's too bad.	tall short fat thin young old	He's/She's short. He/She isn't tall.	short e bed egg pen vet
	Review of Units 7–9					
	Cross-curricular 3: Food rice paddy plant orange grove potato field cow pasture animal **Project Time: Food Collage**					
10	Around Town	Occupations	What's your telephone number? It's 765-1234. Pardon me? 765-1234.	doctor nurse police officer teacher mail carrier firefighter	Is he a doctor? Yes, he is. Is she a doctor? No, she isn't. She's a nurse.	short i dig in pin sit
11	In Annie's Yard	Actions	Dad, this is my friend, Joe. Nice to meet you, Joe. Hello.	ride a bike climb a tree drive a car draw a picture play basketball sing a song	I/You/He/She/It can climb a tree. I/You/He/She/It can't ride a bike.	short o hot mop on pot
12	At the Park	Actions	I'm going now. Bye-bye! See you tomorrow.	swim use a fork fly a kite make a sandwich do a cartwheel play the guitar	Can you/he/she/it swim? Yes, I/he/she/it can. No, I/he/she/it can't.	short u bus nut sun up
	Review of Units 10–12					
	Cross-curricular 4: Trees soil seed root trunk branch leaf **Project Time: Draw a Tree**					

Classroom Language

CD1 1 Listen and do the actions.

The Alphabet

A. CD1 2 Listen and sing along.

A a   B b   C c   D d

E e   F f   G g   H h

I i   J j   K k   L l

M m   N n   O o   P p

Q q   R r   S s   T t

U u   V v   W w

X x   Y y   Z z

B. Point to the letters. Say the alphabet on your own.

In the Neighborhood

Conversation Time

A. CD1 3 Listen and repeat.

Good morning.

Hello! How are you?

Fine, thank you.

B. CD1 4 Listen and find the speakers.

C. Role-play the conversation with a partner.

D. CD1 5 Review. Listen and repeat.

Hello!

Hi!

Word Time

A. 🔘 CD1 6 Listen and repeat.

1.   Annie
2. Ted
3.  Digger
4.  girl
5.  boy
6. dog

B. 🔘 CD1 7 Listen and write the letter.

C. Point and say the words.

D. 🔘 CD1 8 Listen and point.

E. Write the words.
(See pages 70–74.)

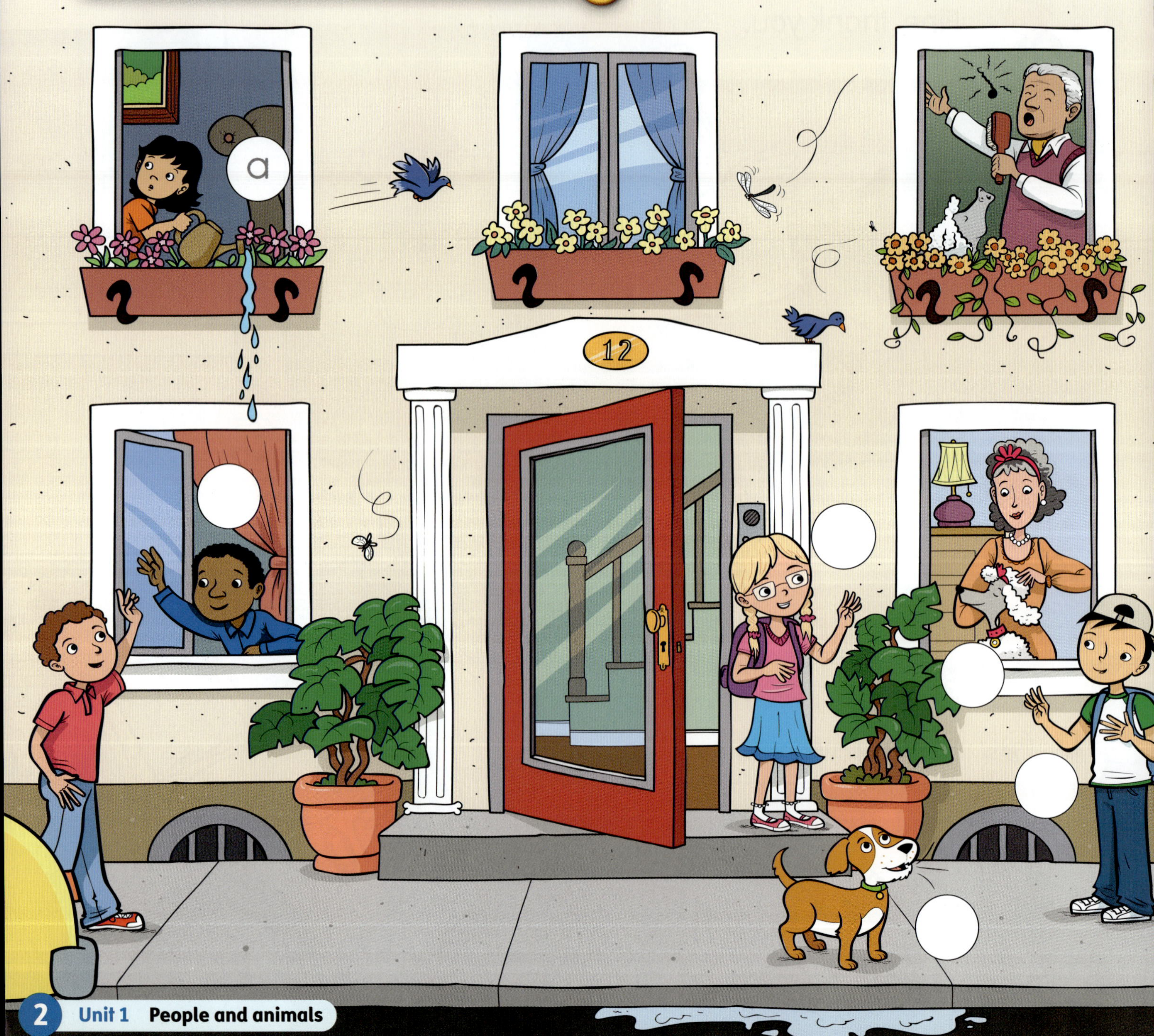

12

A. 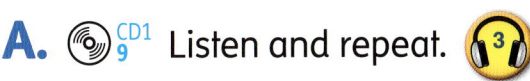 Listen and repeat.

I'm	Annie. a girl.

I'm = I am

You're	Ted. a boy.

You're = You are

B. Listen and repeat. Then practice with a partner.

1. I'm Annie. I'm a girl.

2. You're Ted. You're a boy.

3. I'm Ted. I'm a boy.

4. You're Annie. You're a girl.

5. I'm Digger. I'm a dog.

6. You're Digger. You're a dog.

C. Look at page 2. Point to the picture and practice with a partner.

D. **SONG** Listen and sing along. (See "The Ted and Annie Song" on page 65.)

A. 🔊 CD1 12 Listen and repeat. 🎧⑤

Bb　　**b**all　　**b**ird　　**b**oy

Pp　　**p**encil　　**p**oint　　**p**izza

B. 🔊 CD1 13 Does it begin with **b**? Listen and circle.

1. 　　2. 　　3. 　　4.

C. 🔊 CD1 14 Does it begin with **p**? Listen and circle.

1. 　　2. 　　3. 　　4.

D. 🔊 CD1 15 Does it begin with **b** or **p**? Listen and circle.

1. 　2. 　3. 　4. 　5. 　6.

b p　　b p　　b p　　b p　　b p　　b p

In the Meadow

Conversation Time

A. CD1 16 Listen and repeat.

Ah-choo!

Bless you!

Thanks.

B. CD1 17 Listen and find the speakers.

C. Role-play the conversation with a partner.

D. CD1 18 Review. Listen and repeat.

Hi. I'm Walt.

Hello, Walt!

Word Time

A.  CD1 19 Listen and repeat.

1. tree
2. butterfly
3. flower
4. cloud
5. bird
6. lake

B. CD1 20 Listen and write the letter.

C. Point and say the words.

D. CD1 21 Listen and point.

E. Write the words.
(See pages 70–74.)

A. CD1 22 Listen and repeat. 🎧8

This is	a butterfly.

That's	a bird.

That's = That is

B. CD1 23 Listen and repeat. Then practice with a partner.

1. This is a butterfly.

2. That's a lake.

3. This is a bird.

4. This is a flower.

5. That's a tree.

6. That's a cloud.

C. Look at page 6. Point to the picture and practice with a partner.

D. CD1 24 SONG 🎵 Listen and sing along. 🎧9
(See "This Is a Flower" on page 65.)

A. CD1 25 Listen and repeat. 10

Gg

garden

girl

gorilla

Kk

kangaroo

key

kite

B. CD1 26 Does it begin with **g** or **k**? Listen and circle.

1.

g   k

2.

g   k

3.

g   k

4.

g   k

5.

g   k

6.

g   k

C. CD1 27 Does it begin with **b**, **p**, **g**, or **k**? Listen and write.

1. _____   2. _____   3. _____   4. _____   5. _____   6. _____

On the Farm

Conversation Time

A. 🔘 CD1 28 Listen and repeat.

 Sh! Be quiet!

 Sorry.

 That's okay.

B. 🔘 CD1 29 Listen and find the speakers.

C. Role-play the conversation with a partner.

D. 🔘 CD1 30 Review. Listen and repeat.

Hello! How are you?

Fine, thanks.

A. 🔊 CD1 31 Listen and repeat.

1. goat
2. cow
3. horse
4. chicken
5. sheep
6. cat

B. 🔊 CD1 32 Listen and write the letter.

C. Point and say the words.

D. 🔊 CD1 33 Listen and point.

E. Write the words.
(See pages 70–74.)

A. CD1 34 Listen and repeat.

| **What's** | **this?** **that?** | | **It's** | **a goat.** **a cow.** |

What's = What is

It's = It is

B. CD1 35 Listen and repeat. Then practice with a partner.

1. **What's this?**
   It's a goat.

2. **What's that?**
   It's a horse.

3. **What's that?**
   It's a cat.

4. **What's this?**
   It's a cow.

5. **What's this?**
   It's a chicken.

6. **What's that?**
   It's a sheep.

C. Look at page 10. Point to the picture and practice with a partner.

D. CD1 36 **SONG ♫** Listen and sing along.
(See "What's This?" on page 65.)

A. (CD1 37) Listen and repeat. 🎧15

milk

mop

mother

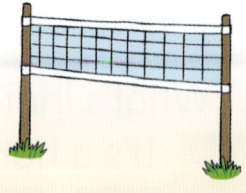
net

night

nurse

B. (CD1 38) Does it begin with **m** or **n**? Listen and match.

1.
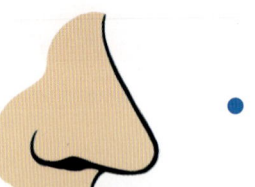

2.

m

3.

4.

n

5.

6.

C. (CD1 39) Does it begin with **m** or **n**? Listen and circle.

1.  m n
2.  m n
3.  m n
4.  m n
5.  m n
6.  m n

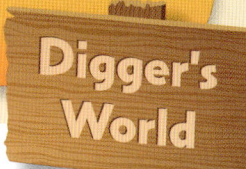

Digger's World

A. CD1 40 Listen and repeat.

1. Good morning! I'm Max.
   Hi! I'm Digger.

2. How are you, Max?
   Fine, thanks.

3. What's that?
   It's a pen.

4. What's this?
   It's a bird.

5. Ah-choo!
   Bless you!
   Thank you.

6. Sh! Be quiet!
   Sorry.
   To be continued...

B. CD1 41 Look at **A**. Listen and point.   **C.** Role-play these scenes.

A. CD1 42 Listen. Find and number the pictures in the puzzle.

dog   tree   cloud   bird   goat   cow   horse   chicken   sheep   cat

B. CD1 43 Listen and circle the correct word.

1.   pizza ball   2.   kite gorilla   3.   milk nose

4.   key girl   5.   mop net   6.   goat boy

C. CD1 44 Listen and find the picture. Write the number.

A. What's that? It's a bug. How many bugs?

B. 🎧 CD1 45 Listen and repeat.

C. 🎧 CD1 46 Listen and read.

1. bee

This is a bee.

2. caterpillar

This is a caterpillar.

3. fly

What's this? It's a fly.

4. spider

What's that? It's a spider.

D. Is it true? Write ✓ or ✗.

1. Look at picture 1. It's a bee. ☐   2. Look at picture 2. It's a spider. ☐

3. Look at picture 3. It's a fly. ☐   4. Look at picture 4. It's a caterpillar. ☐

E. Write the words. (See pages 70–74.)

A. Draw. Ask and answer with a partner.

What's this?

It's a fly.

B. Make a bugs poster.

1. Draw or find pictures of bugs.

2. Write.

3. Share your poster.

This is my poster. It's a bee.

Conversation Time

A. 🎧 CD1 47 Listen and repeat.

Here you are.

Thanks.

You're welcome.

B. 🎧 CD1 48 Listen and find the speakers.

C. Role-play the conversation with a partner.

D. 🎧 CD1 49 Review. Listen and repeat.

Sh! Be quiet!

Sorry.

A. 🔊 CD1 50 Listen and repeat.

1. pen   2. book

3. eraser   4. pencil

5. ruler   6. pencil case

B. 🔊 CD1 51 Listen and write the letter.

C. Point and say the words.

D. 🔊 CD1 52 Listen and point.

E. Write the words.
(See pages 70–74.)

A. 🔊 CD1 53 Listen and repeat.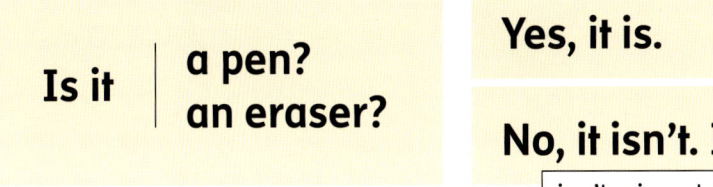

| Is it | a pen? | Yes, it is. |
| an eraser? | | No, it isn't. It's | a pencil. |

isn't = is not   It's = It is

B. 🔊 CD1 54 Listen and repeat. Then practice with a partner.

1. Is it a pen?
   Yes, it is.

2. Is it an eraser?
   No, it isn't. It's a ruler.

3. Is it a book?
   Yes, it is.

4. Is it a pencil case?
   Yes, it is.

5. Is it a pen?
   No, it isn't. It's a pencil.

6. Is it a ruler?
   No, it isn't. It's an eraser.

C. Look at page 18. Point to the picture and practice with a partner.

D. 🔊 CD1 55 SONG ♫ Listen and sing along.
(See "Thanks. You're Welcome." on page 66.)

A.  CD1 56 Listen and repeat. 🎧 20

desk

dog

duck

table

teacher

tiger

B. CD1 57 Does it begin with **d** or **t**? Listen and write.

1.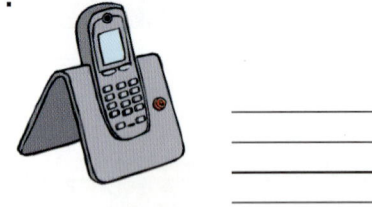
_____

2.
_____

3.
_____

4.
_____

5.
_____

6.
_____

C. CD1 58 Listen and match.

 1

 2

 3

 4

 5

 6

 d

 p

 g

 k

 b

 t

A. 🎧 CD1 59 Listen and repeat.

What's your first name?

Emily.

What's your last name?

Young.

B. 🎧 CD1 60 Listen and find the speakers.

C. Role-play the conversation with a partner.

D. 🎧 CD1 61 Review. Listen and repeat.

Here you are.

Thank you.

Word Time

A. CD1 62 Listen and repeat.

1. one
•

2. two
• •

3. three
• • •

4. four
• • • •

5. five
• • • • •

6. six
• • • • • •

7. seven
• • • •
• • •

8. eight
• • • •
• • • •

9. nine
• • • • •
• • • •

10. ten
• • • • •
• • • • •

11. eleven
• • • • • •
• • • • •

12. twelve
• • • • • •
• • • • • •

B. Find the items in the large scene. Count and write the number.

a. __ ✏

b. __ 🌲

c. __ 🐱

d. __ 🖊

e. __ 🐄

f. __ ☁

g. __ 🐐

h. __ 📙

i. __ 🧢

j. __ 🐦

k. __ 🌷

l. __ 🐕

C. CD1 63 Look at **B**. Listen and check.

D. CD1 64 Listen and point.

E. Write the words. (See pages 70–74.)

A. CD1 65 Listen and repeat.

How many	cows?

| One | cow. |
| Two | cows. |

B. CD1 66 Listen and repeat. Then practice with a partner.

1. How many cows?
   One cow.

2. How many goats?
   Three goats.

3. How many cats?
   Four cats.

4. How many clouds?
   Seven clouds.

5. How many books?
   Ten books.

6. How many pens?
   Twelve pens.

C. Look at page 22. Point to the picture and practice with a partner.

D. CD1 67 **SONG** ♫ Listen and chant.
(See "The Counting Chant" on page 66.)

A. 🎧 CD1 68 Listen and repeat. 🎧 25

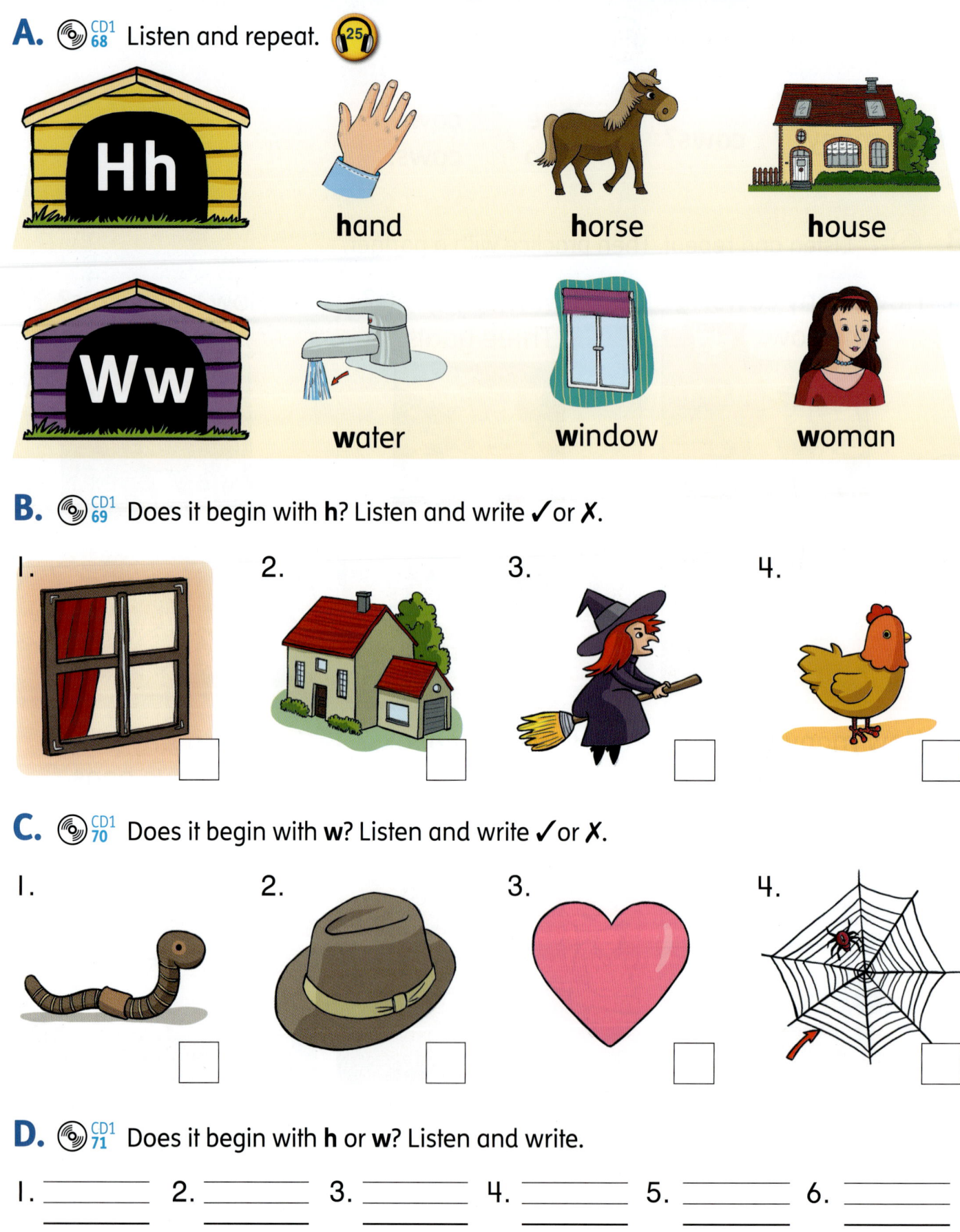

hand

horse

house

water

window

woman

B. 💿 CD1 69 Does it begin with **h**? Listen and write ✓ or ✗.

1.

2.

3.

4.

C. 💿 CD1 70 Does it begin with **w**? Listen and write ✓ or ✗.

1.

2.

3.

4.

D. 💿 CD1 71 Does it begin with **h** or **w**? Listen and write.

1. _____
2. _____
3. _____
4. _____
5. _____
6. _____

In Gym Class

Conversation Time

A. 🎧 CD1 72 Listen and repeat.

Ouch!

Are you okay?

I think so.

B. 🎧 CD1 73 Listen and find the speakers.

C. Role-play the conversation with a partner.

D. 🎧 CD1 74 Review. Listen and repeat.

That's okay.

Sorry!

A. 🎧 CD1 75 Listen and repeat.

1. happy
2. sad
3. cold
4. hot
5. hungry
6. thirsty

B. 🎧 CD1 76 Listen and write the letter.

C. Point and say the words.

D. 🎧 CD1 77 Listen and point.

E. Write the words.
(See pages 70–74.)

Practice Time

A. CD1 78 Listen and repeat.

Are you	happy?

Yes, I am.

No, I'm not. I'm | **sad.**

I'm = I am

B. CD1 79 Listen and repeat. Then practice with a partner.

1. Are you happy?
   Yes, I am.

2. Are you happy?
   No, I'm not. I'm sad.

3. Are you cold?
   Yes, I am.

4. Are you cold?
   No, I'm not. I'm hot.

5. Are you thirsty?
   Yes, I am.

6. Are you thirsty?
   No, I'm not. I'm hungry.

C. Look at page 26. Point to the picture and practice with a partner.

D. CD1 80 **SONG** 🎵 Listen and sing along.
(See "Are You Happy?" on page 67.)

A.  CD1 81 Listen and repeat.

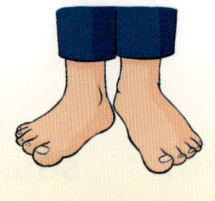

feet

fish

fork

van

vase

violin

B. CD1 82 Do they both begin with the same sound? Listen and write ✓ or ✗.

1.

2.

3.

4.

5.

6.

C. CD1 83 Does it begin with **f**, **m**, **n**, or **v**? Listen and circle.

1.  f v

2. m n

3.  f v

4. m n

5.  f v

6.  m n

Digger's World

A. CD1 84 Listen and repeat.

1. Are you hungry, Max?
Yes, I am.

2. Here you are.
Thanks.
You're welcome.

3. Are you thirsty, Max?
Yes, I am.

4. Here you are.
Thanks.
You're welcome.

5. I'm happy!

6. Are you okay?
No, I'm not.
Oh, Max!
To be continued...

B. CD1 85 Look at **A**. Listen and point.

C. Role-play these scenes.

A. 🔊 CD1 86 Count the items. Write the number in each box.
Then listen and check.

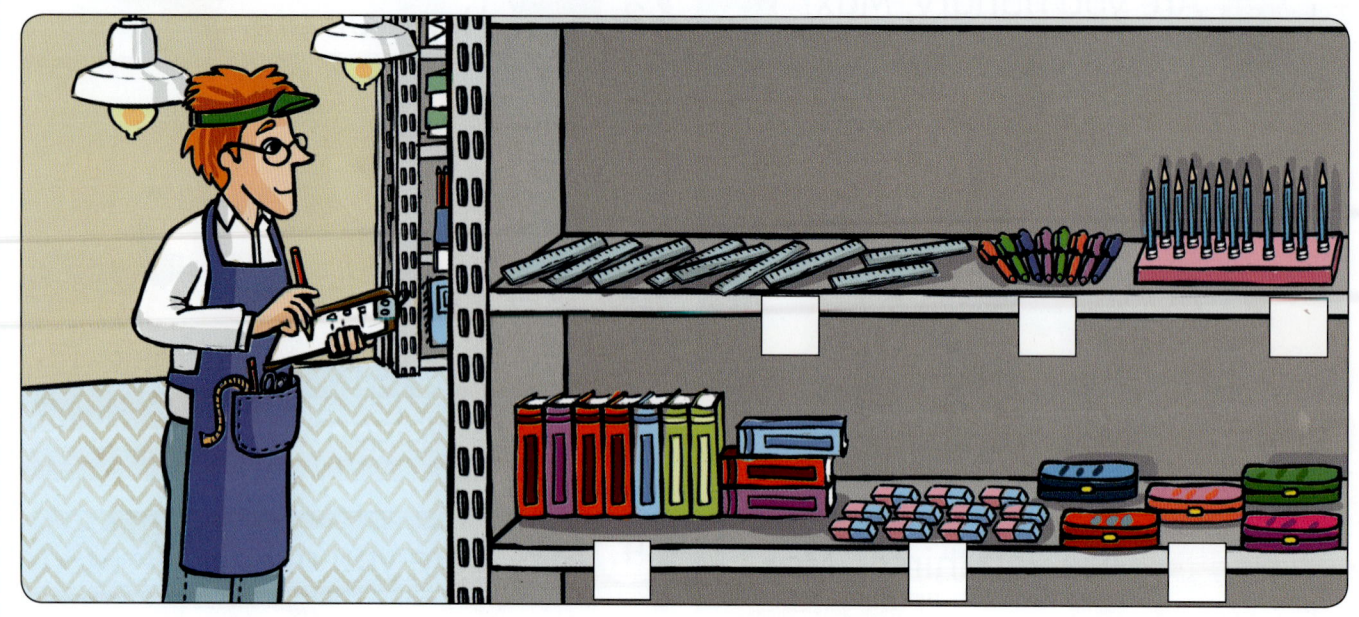

B. 🔊 CD1 87 Listen and write the numbers.

1. _____ 2. _____ 3. _____ 4. _____ 5. _____ 6. _____

C. 🔊 CD1 88 Listen and circle the correct word.

1. desk   tiger   2. house   water   3. fish   van

4. woman   horse   5. violin   feet   6. table   duck

D. 🔊 CD1 89 Listen and circle ✓ or ✗.

1. ✓   ✗   2. ✓   ✗   3. ✓   ✗   4. ✓   ✗

A. How many numbers do you know?

B. 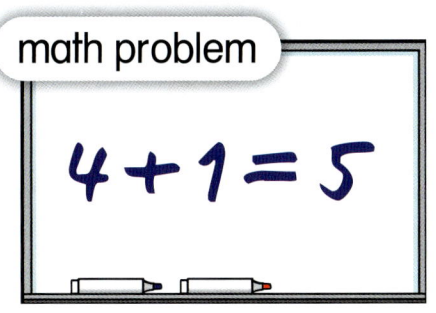 CD1 90 Listen and repeat.

C. CD1 91 Listen and read.

math problem

$4 + 1 = 5$

This is a math problem.

plus   equals

Three   plus   one   equals   four.

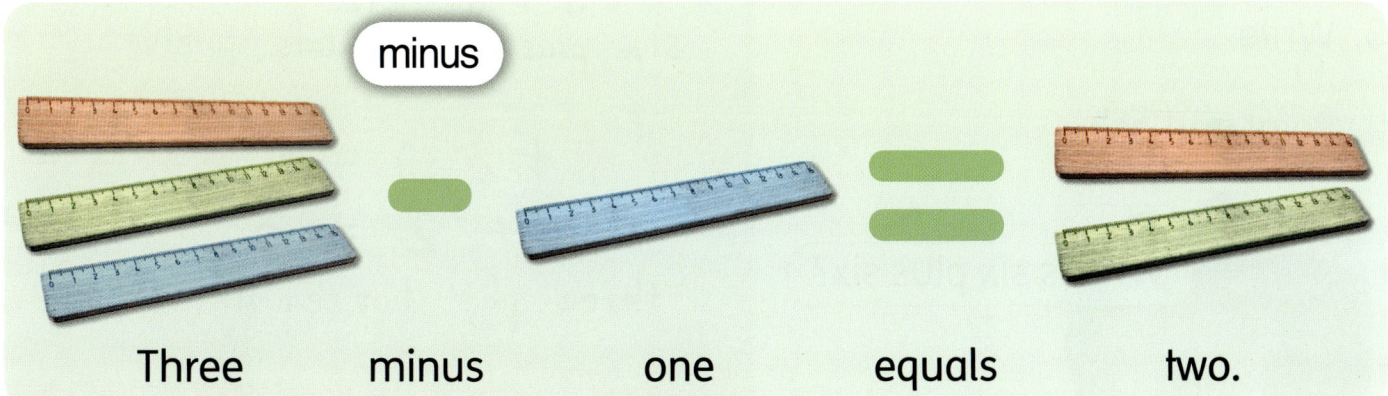

minus

Three   minus   one   equals   two.

D. Read and match.

1. Two plus eight equals •   • eight.
2. Twelve minus three equals •   • ten.
3. Ten minus two equals •   • eleven.
4. Six plus five equals •   • nine.

E. Write the words. (See pages 70–74.)

A. Write four math problems. Ask and answer with a partner.

What's four plus two?

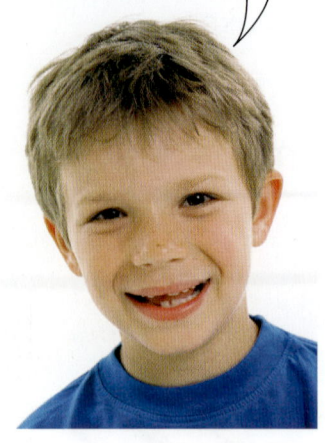

$4 + 2 =$
$6 - 3 =$
$10 + 1 =$
$9 - 5 =$

Four plus two equals six.

B. Make a math problems poster.

1. Think of four math problems.

2. Draw or find pictures.

3. Write.

4. Point and ask.

What's six plus six?

Math Problems

$6 + 6 = 12$
Six plus six equals twelve.

$3 + 2 = 5$
three plus two equals five.

$10 - 6 = 4$
ten minus six equals four.

$7 - 5 = 2$
seven minus five equals two.

At the Food Court

A.  CD2 1 Listen and repeat.

 Are you finished?

 No, not yet.

 Please hurry!

B. CD2 2 Listen and find the speakers.

C. Role-play the conversation with a partner.

D. CD2 3 Review. Listen and repeat.

I'm hungry. Are you hungry?

Yes, I am.

Word Time

A. 🔘 CD2 4 Listen and repeat.

1. 🍔 burgers
2. 🥗 salad
3. 🍚 rice
4. 🐟 fish
5. 🍝 spaghetti
6. 🍕 pizza

B. 🔘 CD2 5 Listen and write the letter.

C. Point and say the words.

D. 🔘 CD2 6 Listen and point.

E. Write the words.
(See pages 70–74.)

32

A. CD2 7 Listen and repeat.

I You	like	burgers.

I You	don't like	pizza.

don't = do not

B. CD2 8 Listen and repeat. Then practice with a partner.

1. I like burgers.

2. I don't like salad.

3. You don't like rice.

4. You like spaghetti.

5. You like fish.

6. I don't like pizza.

C. Look at page 34. Point to the picture and practice with a partner.

D. CD2 9 **SONG** ♫ Listen and sing along.
(See "I Like Pizza" on page 67.)

A. 🎧 CD2 10 Listen and repeat. 🎧 35

Ss

sea

sock

soup

Zz

zebra

zipper

zoo

B. 🎧 CD2 11 Does it begin with **s**? Listen and circle.

1.

2.

3.

4.

C. 🎧 CD2 12 Does it begin with **z**? Listen and circle.

1.

2.

3.

4.

D. 🎧 CD2 13 Does it begin with **f**, **s**, **v**, or **z**? Listen and write.

1. _____ 2. _____ 3. _____ 4. _____ 5. _____ 6. _____

At the Supermarket

8

Conversation Time

A. CD2 14 Listen and repeat.

May I borrow a pen?

Sure. Here you are.

Thanks.

B. CD2 15 Listen and find the speakers.

C. Role-play the conversation with a partner.

D. CD2 16 Review. Listen and repeat.

What's that?

It's pizza.

Word Time

A. CD2 17 Listen and repeat.

1. apples
2. oranges
3. bananas
4. cucumbers
5. potatoes
6. carrots

B. CD2 18 Listen and write the letter.

C. Point and say the words.

D. CD2 19 Listen and point.

E. Write the words.
(See pages 70–74.)

37

Practice Time

A. CD2 20 Listen and repeat.

Do you like	apples?

Yes, I do.

No, I don't.

don't = do not

B. CD2 21 Listen and repeat. Then practice with a partner.

1. Do you like apples?
   Yes, I do.

2. Do you like carrots?
   No, I don't.

3. Do you like oranges?
   Yes, I do.

4. Do you like cucumbers?
   Yes, I do.

5. Do you like bananas?
   No, I don't.

6. Do you like potatoes?
   No, I don't.

C. Look at page 38. Point to the picture and practice with a partner.

D. CD2 22 **SONG** ♫ Listen and sing along.
(See "Yum! Yum! Yum!" on page 68.)

A. 🎧 CD2 23 Listen and repeat. 🎧 40

| ant | bag | hat | map |

B. 🎧 CD2 24 Does it have **short a**? Listen and circle ✓ or ✗.

1.   2.   3.   4.   5.

| ✓   ✗ | ✓   ✗ | ✓   ✗ | ✓   ✗ | ✓   ✗ |

C. Read the words with your teacher.

1.
-a-
-ad

bad
dad
mad

2.
-a-
-ag

nag
tag
wag

3.
-a-
-an

fan
man
pan

4.
-a-
-at

bat
hat
pat

D. 🎧 CD2 25 Look at **C**. Listen and point to the words.

E. 🎧 CD2 26 Does it have **short a**? Listen and write ✓ or ✗.

1. ☐   2. ☐   3. ☐   4. ☐   5. ☐   6. ☐

At the Circus

Conversation Time

A. CD2 27 Listen and repeat.

What's wrong?

I feel sick.

That's too bad.

B. CD2 28 Listen and find the speakers.

C. Role-play the conversation with a partner.

D. CD2 29 Review. Listen and repeat.

Are you okay?

I think so.

Word Time

42

A. 🔊 CD2 30 Listen and repeat.

1.  tall
2. short
3. fat
4. thin
5. young
6. old

B. 🔊 CD2 31 Listen and write the letter.

C. Point and say the words.

D. 🔊 CD2 32 Listen and point.

E. Write the words.
(See pages 70–74.)

Practice Time

A. CD2 33 Listen and repeat. 🎧43

He's She's	short.	He isn't She isn't	tall.

He's = He is | She's = She is

isn't = is not

B. CD2 34 Listen and repeat. Then practice with a partner.

1. He's short.
   He isn't tall.

2. She's fat.
   She isn't thin.

3. He's old.
   He isn't young.

4. He's thin.
   He isn't fat.

5. She's tall.
   She isn't short.

6. She's young.
   She isn't old.

C. Look at page 42. Point to the picture and practice with a partner.

D. CD2 35 **SONG** 🎵 Listen and chant.
(See "The Tall/Short Chant" on page 68.)

A. CD2 36 Listen and repeat.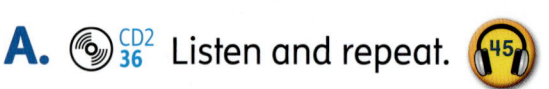

short e

bed   **e**gg   pen   ve**t**

B. CD2 37 Does it have **short e**? Listen and circle ✓ or ✗.

1.   2.   3.   4.   5.

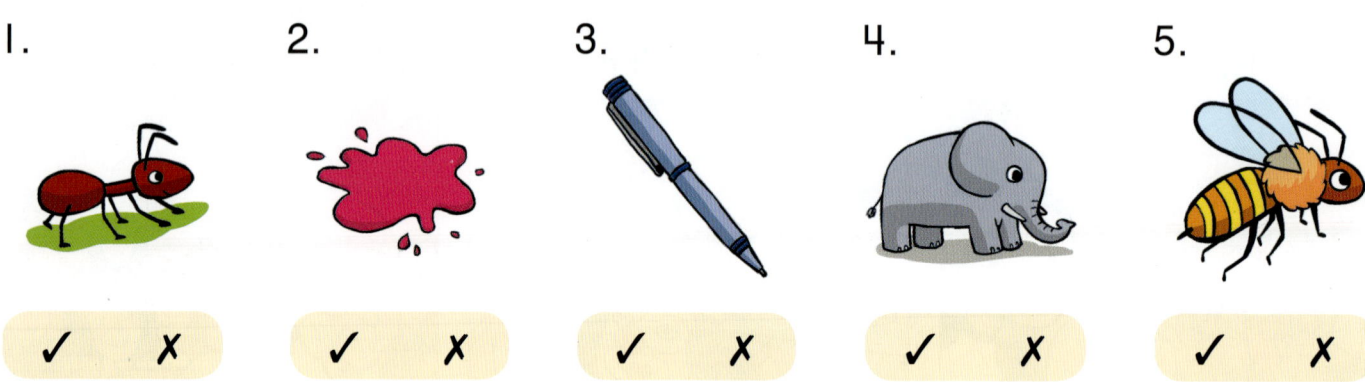

| ✓   ✗ | ✓   ✗ | ✓   ✗ | ✓   ✗ | ✓   ✗ |

C. Read the words with your teacher.

1.	2.	3.	4.
-e- **-ed**	**-e-** **-en**	**-e-** **-eg**	**-e-** **-et**
bed fed Ted	hen men ten	beg Meg peg	net pet set

D. CD2 38 Look at **C**. Listen and point to the words.

E. CD2 39 Does it have **short a** or **short e**? Listen and circle.

1.   2.   3.   4.   5.   6.

a e   a e   a e   a e   a e   a e

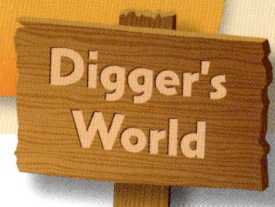

A. CD2 40 Listen and repeat.

B. CD2 41 Look at **A**. Listen and point.   **C.** Role-play these scenes.

A. 🎧 CD2 42 Listen and write ✓ or ✗.

I like... (✓)   I don't like... (✗)

B. 🎧 CD2 43 Listen and circle the correct word.

1. soup   zoo   2. ant   egg   3. bag   bed

4. pen   map   5. zebra   sock   6. vet   hat

C. 🎧 CD2 44 Listen and find the picture. Write the number.

A. What foods can you see?

B. ⊚ CD2 45 Listen and repeat.

C. ⊚ CD2 46 Listen and read.

1. rice paddy

plant

What's this?
It's a rice paddy.

2. orange grove

This is an orange grove.
Do you like oranges?

3. potato field

Is it an orange grove?
No, it isn't. It's a potato field.

4. cow pasture

animal

And this is a cow pasture.
How many cows?

D. Read and match.

1. Look at picture 1. It's a rice •   • pasture.

2. Look at picture 4. It's a cow •   • grove.

3. Look at picture 3. It's a potato •   • field.

4. Look at picture 2. It's an orange •   • paddy.

E. Write the words. (See pages 70–74.)

A. Choose foods. Ask and answer with a partner.

I like apples.
Do you like apples?

No, I don't.

B. Make a food collage.

1. Think of foods from animals and plants.

2. Draw or find pictures.

3. Write.

4. Share your collage.

This is milk.
I like milk.

10

A.  Listen and repeat.

 What's your telephone number?

 It's 765–1234.

 Pardon me?

 765–1234.

B. CD2 48 Listen and find the speakers.

C. Role-play the conversation with a partner.

D. CD2 49 Review. Listen and repeat.

Please hurry!

Okay, okay!

Word Time

A. 🎵 CD2 50 Listen and repeat.

1.  doctor

2.  nurse

3.  police officer

4.  teacher

5.  mail carrier

6.  firefighter

B. 🎵 CD2 51 Listen and write the letter.

C. Point and say the words.

D. 🎵 CD2 52 Listen and point.

E. Write the words.
(See pages 70–74.)

Practice Time

A. CD2 53 Listen and repeat.

Is	he she	a doctor?

Yes,	he she	is.

No,	he she	isn't.	He's She's	a nurse.

is not = isn't   He's = He is   She's = She is

B. CD2 54 Listen and repeat. Then practice with a partner.

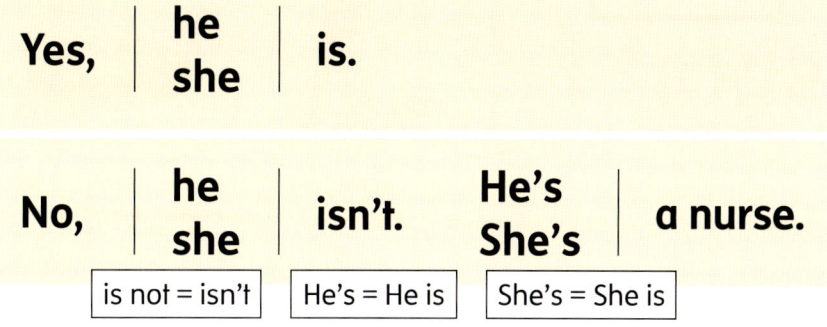

1. Is he a doctor?
   Yes, he is.

2. Is she a doctor?
   No, she isn't. She's a nurse.

3. Is he a police officer?
   Yes, he is.

4. Is she a police officer?
   No, she isn't. She's a firefighter.

5. Is he a mail carrier?
   Yes, he is.

6. Is she a mail carrier?
   No, she isn't. She's a teacher.

C. Look at page 50. Point to the picture and practice with a partner.

D. CD2 55 **SONG** ♫ Listen and sing along.
(See "The Work Song" on page 68.)

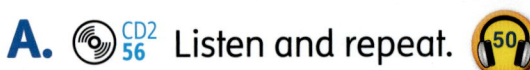

Phonics Time

A. 🔘 CD2 56 Listen and repeat. 🎧 50

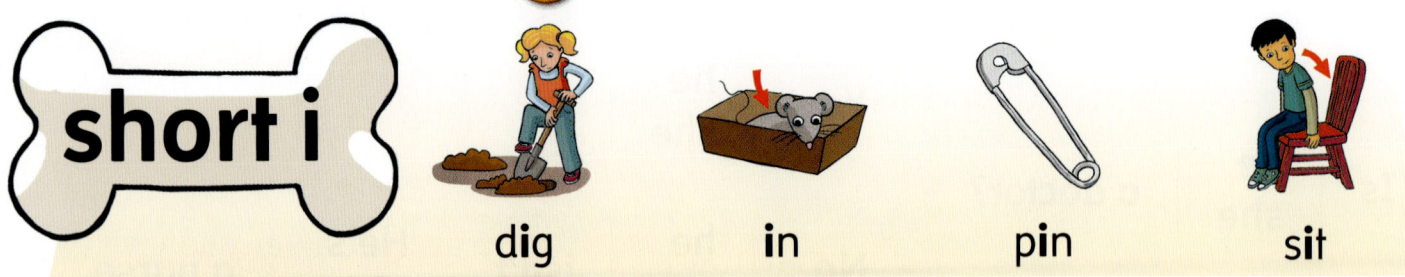

short i   dig   in   pin   sit

B. 🔘 CD2 57 Do they both have **short i**? Listen and write ✓ or ✗.

1. ☐
2. ☐
3. ☐
4. ☐
5. ☐
6. ☐

C. Read the words with your teacher.

1. -i- -ig	2. -i- -in	3. -i- -ip	4. -i- -it
big fig wig	fin tin win	dip hip zip	hit pit sit

D. 🔘 CD2 58 Look at **C**. Listen and point to the words.

E. 🔘 CD2 59 Does it have **short a**, **short e**, or **short i**? Listen and circle.

1. e i
2. a e
3. a e
4. e i
5. a e
6. e i

11 In Annie's Yard

Conversation Time

A. 🔊 CD2 60 Listen and repeat.

Dad, this is my friend, Sam.

Nice to meet you, Sam.

Hello.

B. 🔊 CD2 61 Listen and find the speakers.

C. Role-play the conversation with two other students.

D. 🔊 CD2 62 Review. Listen and repeat.

Are you finished?

No, not yet.

Word Time

A. 🔘 CD2 63 Listen and repeat.

1.   ride a bike

2.  climb a tree

3.  drive a car

4.  draw a picture

5.  play basketball

6.  sing a song

B. 🔘 CD2 64 Listen and write the letter.

C. Point and say the words.

D. 🔘 CD2 65 Listen and point.

E. Write the words. (See pages 70–74.)

A. CD2 66 Listen and repeat. 53

I		
You		
He	can	climb a tree.
She		
It		

I		
You		
He	can't	ride a bike.
She		
It		

can't = cannot

B. CD2 67 Listen and repeat. Then practice with a partner.

1. It can't climb a tree.
2. You can play basketball.

3. I can't drive a car.
4. She can draw a picture.

5. He can't ride a bike.
6. It can sing a song.

C. Look at page 54. Point to the picture and practice with a partner.

D. CD2 68 **SONG** 🎵 Listen and sing along. (See "She Can Ride a Bike" on page 69.) 54

A. ⊚ CD2 69 Listen and repeat. 🎧 55

short o

hot   mop   on   pot

B. ⊚ CD2 70 Does it have **short a**, **short e**, **short i**, or **short o**? Listen and circle.

1.   2.   3.   4.   5.

e o   i o   a o   a o   e o

C. Read the words with your teacher.

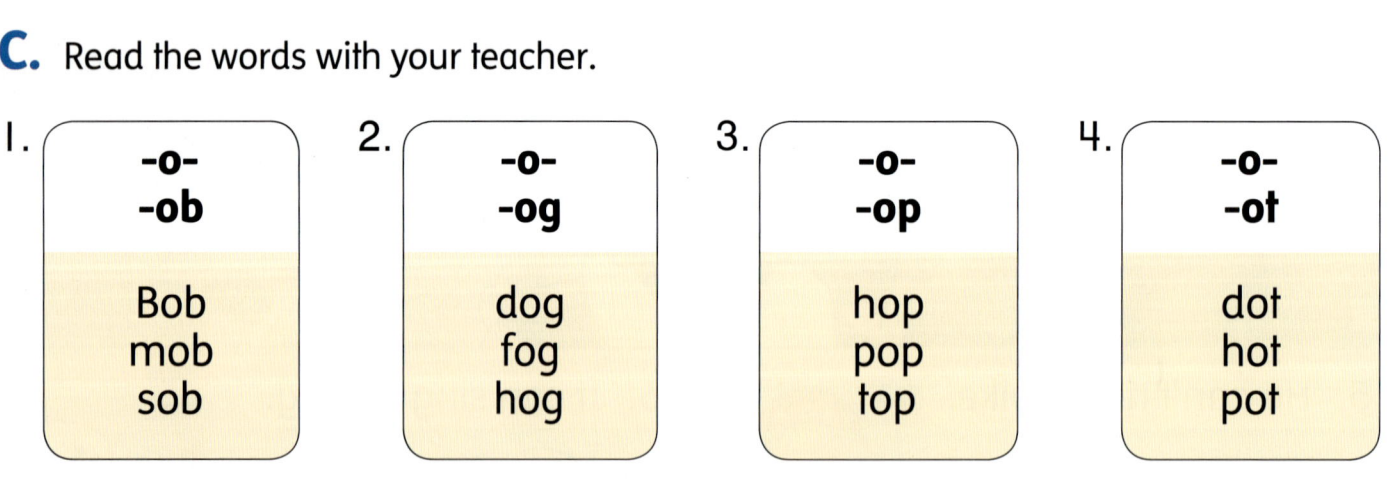

1. -o- -ob	2. -o- -og	3. -o- -op	4. -o- -ot
Bob mob sob	dog fog hog	hop pop top	dot hot pot

D. ⊚ CD2 71 Look at **C**. Listen and point to the words.

E. ⊚ CD2 72 Does it have **short o**? Listen and write ✓ or ✗.

1. ☐   2. ☐   3. ☐   4. ☐   5. ☐   6. ☐

At the Park

Conversation Time

A. CD2 73 Listen and repeat.

I'm going now.

Bye-bye!

See you tomorrow.

B. CD2 74 Listen and find the speakers.

C. Role-play the conversation with two other students.

D. CD2 75 Review. Listen and repeat.

Hello!

Hello. Nice to meet you.

Word Time

A. CD2 76 Listen and repeat.

1. swim
2. use a fork
3. fly a kite
4. make a sandwich
5. do a cartwheel
6. play the guitar

B. CD2 77 Listen and write the letter.

C. Point and say the words.

D. CD2 78 Listen and point.

E. Write the words. (See pages 70–74.)

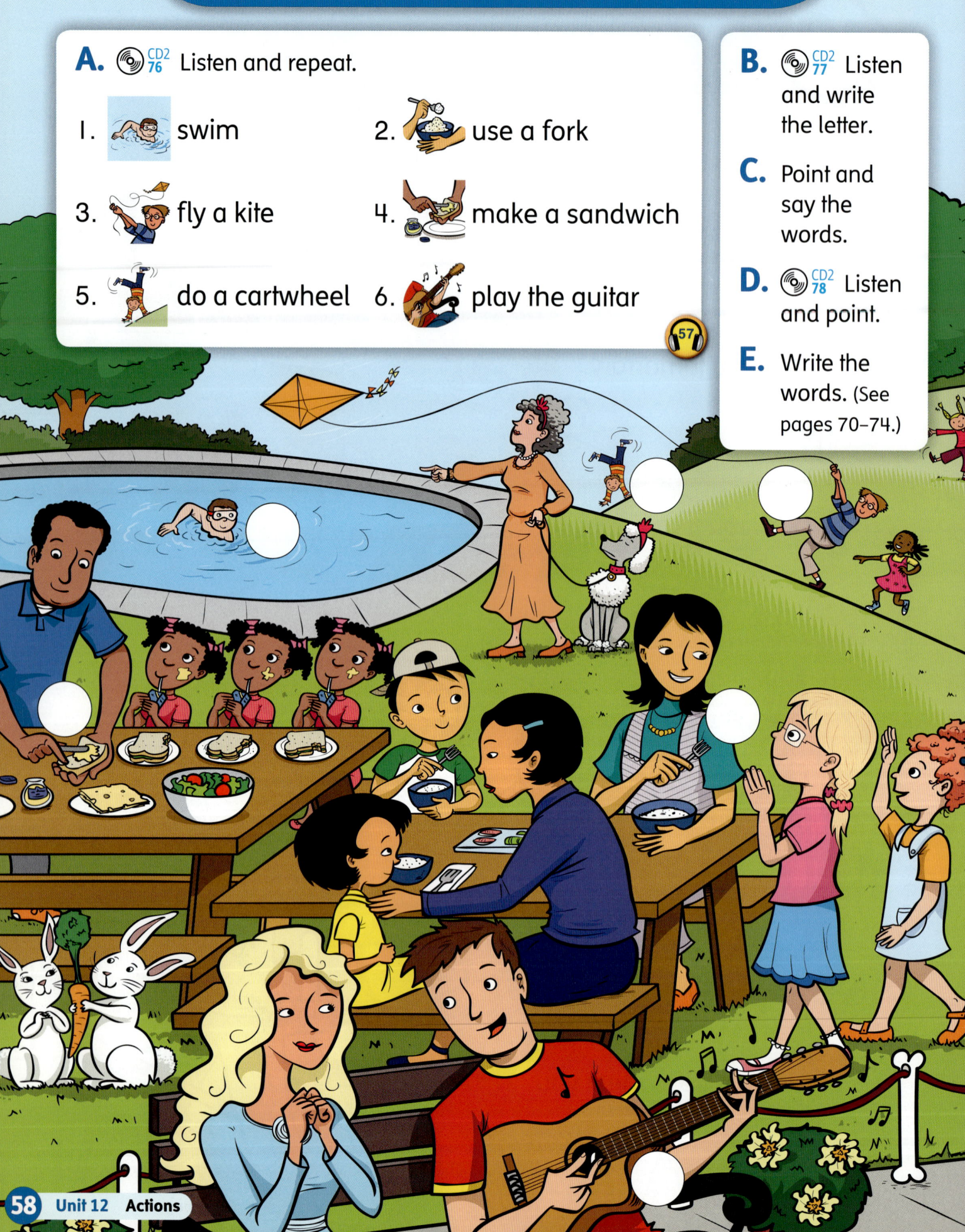

Practice Time

A. 🎧 CD2 79 Listen and repeat.

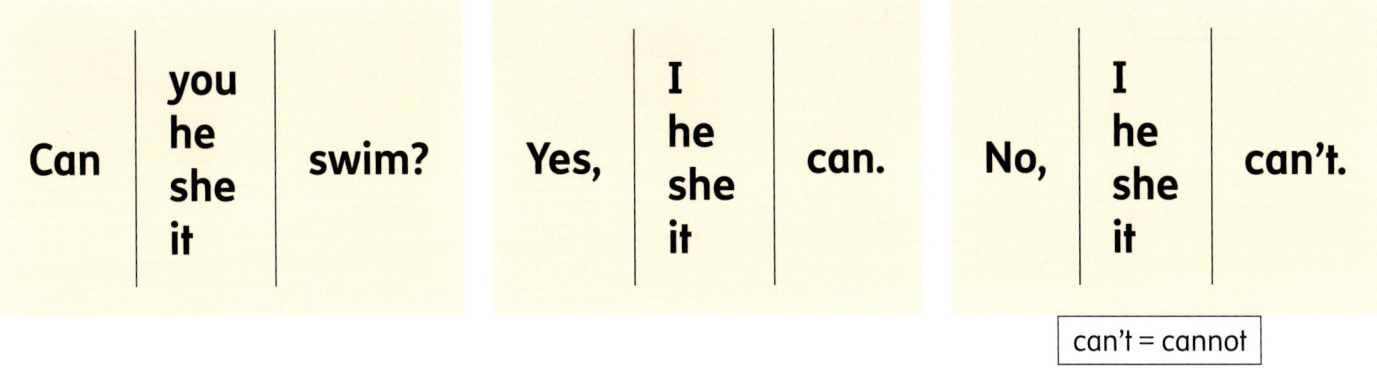

| Can | you
he
she
it | swim? | Yes, | I
he
she
it | can. | No, | I
he
she
it | can't. |

can't = cannot

B. 🎧 CD2 80 Listen and repeat. Then practice with a partner.

1. Can it swim?
   Yes, it can.

2. Can you use a fork?
   No, I can't.

3. Can she fly a kite?
   No, she can't.

4. Can he make a sandwich?
   Yes, he can.

5. Can she do a cartwheel?
   No, she can't.

6. Can you play the guitar?
   Yes, I can.

C. Look at page 58. Point to the picture and practice with a partner.

D. 🎧 CD2 81 **SONG** 🎵 Listen and sing along.
(See "The Kite Song" on page 69.)

A.  CD2 82 Listen and repeat. 60

bus   nut   sun   up

B. CD2 83 Does it have **short u**? Listen and circle.

1.    2.    3.    4.

C. Read the words with your teacher.

1. -u- -ub	2. -u- -ug	3. -u- -um	4. -u- -un
hub	bug	gum	bun
sub	hug	hum	fun
tub	mug	sum	nun

D. CD2 84 Look at **C.** Listen and point to the words.

E. CD2 85 Listen and match.

1   **2**   **3**   **4**   **5**

hat   pen   pin   mop   bus

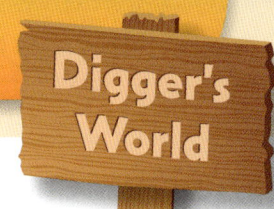

A. CD2 86 Listen and repeat.

1. Max, this is Doc.
I'm a doctor.
Nice to meet you, Doc.

2. What's your last name?
Adams. I'm Max Adams.

3. Ouch!

4. That's Pat. She's a mail carrier.
She can ride a bike.

5. Can you ride a bike?
No, I can't.

6. I'm going now. Bye-bye.
Bye-bye!
See you in level 2!

B. CD2 87 Look at **A**. Listen and point.   **C.** Role-play these scenes.

A. (CD2 88) Listen and ✓ the correct words.

		He	She	can	can't	
1.						ride a bike.
2.						fly a kite.
3.						drive a car.
4.						do a cartwheel.
5.						make a sandwich.

B. (CD2 89) Listen and circle the correct word.

1.   dig   dog   2.   hat   hot   3.   bus   bat

4.   in   on   5.   sun   sit   6.   nut   mop

C. (CD2 90) Listen and circle ✓ or ✗.

1.   2.   3.   4.

✓ ✗   ✓ ✗   ✓ ✗   ✓ ✗

A. Can you climb a tree?

B. 🎧 CD2 91 Listen and repeat.

C. 🎧 CD2 92 Listen and read.

It's soil. Can you see the seed?

Look! It's a root.

This is the trunk.

This is a branch and this is a leaf. It's a tall tree.

D. Read and circle the correct word.

1. Look at picture 1. Look! It's a   leaf | seed.
2. Look at picture 2. I can see the   root | seed.
3. Look at picture 3. It isn't a root. It's a   branch | trunk.
4. Look at picture 4. Is it a   leaf | trunk?   Yes, it is.

E. Write the words. (See pages 70–74.)

A. Draw and cover. Ask and answer with a partner.

Is it a branch?

No, it isn't. It's a trunk.

B. Draw a tree.

1. Draw and write.

2. Share your drawing.

3. Point and ask.

What is it?

leaf

branch

trunk

soil

seed

root

Songs and Chants

 1 The Ted and Annie Song (Melody: Where Is Thumbkin?)

Hi! I'm Annie. Hi! I'm Annie.
I'm a girl. I'm a girl.
   Hi! I'm Ted. Hi! I'm Ted.
   I'm a boy. I'm a boy.

Hi! I'm Annie. Hi! I'm Annie.
   Hi! I'm Ted. Hi! I'm Ted.
How are you today, Ted?
   Fine, thank you, Annie.
   How are you?
Fine, thank you.

 2 This is a Flower (Melody: Jimmy Crack Corn)

This is a flower.
   That's a tree.
This is a flower.
   That's a cloud.
This is a flower.
   That's a bird
   and that's a butterfly!

This is a flower.
   That's a lake.
This is a flower.
   That's a cloud.
This is a flower.
   That's a tree
   and that's a butterfly!

 3 What's This? (Melody: Head, Shoulders, Knees, and Toes)

What's this?
   It's a chicken. It's a chicken.
What's that?
   It's a horse. It's a horse.

   Sh! Be quiet!
Sorry.
   That's okay.
What's that?
   It's a sheep. It's a sheep.

4 Thanks. You're Welcome.

(Melody: Battle Hymn of the Republic)

Is it a pencil case?
　No, it isn't.
Is it a ruler?
　No, it isn't.
Is it an eraser?
　Yes, it is.
Here you are.
　Thanks.
You're welcome.

Is it a pencil?
　No, it isn't.
Is it a book?
　No, it isn't.
Is it a pen?
　Yes, it is.
Here you are.
　Thanks.
You're welcome.

5 The Counting Chant

Pencils, pens, books.
Pencils, pens, books.
How many pencils?
　11 pencils!
How many pens?
　12 pens!
How many books?
　10 books!
Pencils, pens, books.

Cats, dogs, cows.
Cats, dogs, cows.
How many cats?
　4 cats!
How many dogs?
　5 dogs!
How many cows?
　1 cow!
Cats, dogs, cows.

6 Are You Happy?

(Melody: Clementine)

Are you happy?
Are you happy?
Are you happy?
   No, I'm not. *I'm sad.*
Are you cold?
Are you cold?
Are you cold?
   No, I'm not. *I'm hot.*

Are you hungry?
Are you hungry?
Are you hungry?
   No, I'm not. *I'm thirsty.*
Are you sad?
Are you sad?
Are you sad?
   No, I'm not. *I'm happy.*

7 I Like Pizza

(Melody: This Old Man)

I like pizza.
Yes, yes, yes.
   I like burgers.
   Yes, yes, yes.
I don't like salad.
No, no, no.
   I don't like spaghetti.
   No, no, no.

I like fish.
Yes, yes, yes.
   I like rice.
   Yes, yes, yes.
I don't like pizza.
No, no, no.
   I don't like burgers.
   No, no, no.
Are you finished?
   No, not yet.
Please hurry!

Songs and Chants

 8 Yum! Yum! Yum! (Melody: I'm a Little Tea Pot)

Do you like bananas?
  Yes, I do.
  Yes, I do.
  Yum! Yum! Yum!
Do you like apples?
  No, I don't.
  I don't like apples.
  Yuck! Yuck! Yuck!

Do you like potatoes?
  Yes, I do.
  Yes, I do.
  Yum! Yum! Yum!
Do you like carrots?
  No, I don't.
  I don't like carrots.
  Yuck! Yuck! Yuck!

 9 The Tall / Short Chant

She's short.	He's tall.
She isn't tall.	He isn't short.
She's young.	He's young.
She isn't old.	He isn't old.
She's thin.	He's thin.
She isn't fat.	He isn't fat.
She's Annie!	He's Ted!

 10 The Work Song (Melody: La Cucaracha)

Is she a teacher, teacher?
  No, she isn't.
  No, she isn't.
Is she a police officer, police officer?
  No, she isn't.
  She's a doctor.

Is he a mail carrier, mail carrier?
  No, he isn't.
  No, he isn't.
Is he a firefighter, firefighter?
  No, he isn't.
He's a nurse.

11 She Can Ride a Bike

(Melody: The Farmer in the Dell)

She can ride a bike.
She can ride a bike.
She can't play basketball.
She can ride a bike.

He can climb a tree.
He can climb a tree.
He can't play basketball.
He can climb a tree.

She can drive a car.
She can drive a car.
She can't play basketball.
She can drive a car.

He can sing a song.
He can sing a song.
He can't play basketball.
He can sing a song.

 **12 The Kite Song**

(Melody: Oh! Susanna)

Can you fly a kite?
    Yes, I can. I can fly a kite.
Can you play the guitar?
    Yes, I can. I can play the guitar.
    I can fly a kite.
    I can play the guitar.
Can you do a cartwheel?
    No, I can't.
    I can fly a kite.

Can he fly a kite?
    Yes, he can. He can fly a kite.
Can he play the guitar?
    Yes, he can. He can play the guitar.
    He can fly a kite.
    He can play the guitar.
Can he do a cartwheel?
    No, he can't.
    He can fly a kite.

My Picture Dictionary

Write the words.

A a

_____
_____

_____
_____

_____
_____

B b

_____
_____

_____
_____

_____
_____

_____
_____

_____
_____

_____
_____

_____
_____

_____
_____

C c

_____
_____

_____
_____

_____
_____

_____
_____

_____
_____

_____
_____

_____
_____

_____
_____

_____
_____

_____
_____

D d

E e

8

11

=

F f

5

4

G g

H h

(writing lines)

(writing lines)

(writing lines)

(writing lines)

L l

(writing lines)

(writing lines)

M m

(writing lines)

(writing lines)

4 + 1 = 5

(writing lines)

—

(writing lines)

N n

9

(writing lines)

O o

(writing lines)

1

(writing lines)

(writing lines)

(writing lines)

P p

(writing lines)

(writing lines)

(writing lines)

(writing lines)

(writing lines)

R r

T t

U u

Y y

10

3

12

2

A. I can say these sentences.

1. ☐    I'm Annie. I'm a girl.
You're Ted. You're a boy.

2. ☐    This is a bird.
That's a butterfly.

3. ☐    What's this? It's a horse.
What's that? It's a cow.

B. I can say these words.

1. Digger  ☐
2. cat ☐
3. tree ☐
4. flower ☐

5. goat ☐
6. cloud ☐
7. dog ☐
8. lake ☐

C. I can talk about this picture. ☐

D. I can say the sounds of these letters.

b ☐   p ☐   g ☐   k ☐   m ☐   n ☐

A. I can say these sentences.

1. ☐  Is it a pen? No, it isn't. It's a pencil.
Is it a ruler? Yes, it is.

2. ☐  How many books?
Four books.

3. ☐  Are you hot? Yes, I am.
Are you hungry? No, I'm not. I'm thirsty.

B. I can say these words.

1. happy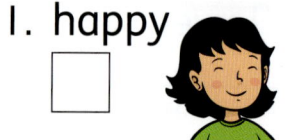
☐

2. ruler
☐

3. eleven
☐

4. cold
☐

5. eraser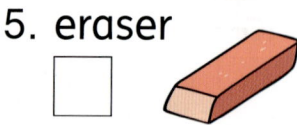
☐

6. twelve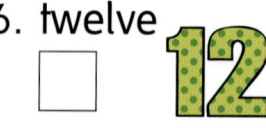
☐

7. sad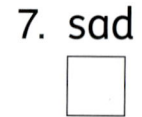
☐

8. pencil case
☐

C. I can talk about this picture. ☐

D. I can say the sounds of these letters.

d ☐   t ☐   h ☐   w ☐   f ☐   v ☐

A. I can say these sentences.

1.
I like bananas.
You don't like apples.

2.
Do you like salad? Yes, I do.
Do you like pizza? No, I don't.

3.
She's young. She isn't old.
He's old. He isn't young.

B. I can say these words.

1. oranges

2. fish

3. tall

4. short

5. carrots

6. burgers

7. potatoes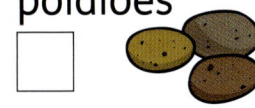

8. rice

C. I can talk about this picture.

D. I can say the sounds of these letters.

s   z

E. I can read these words.

ant   **hat**   **bed**   **egg**

A. I can say these sentences.

1. ☐ Is he a doctor? Yes, he is. Is she a doctor? No, she isn't. She's a mail carrier.

2. ☐ He can ride a bike. I can't ride a bike.

3. ☐ Can you swim? Yes, I can. Can it swim? No, it can't.

B. I can say these words.

1. teacher ☐

2. drive a car ☐

3. fly a kite ☐

4. police officer ☐

5. sing a song ☐

6. make a sandwich ☐

7. firefighter ☐

8. climb a tree ☐

C. I can talk about this picture. ☐

D. I can read these words.

sit ☐   in ☐   mop ☐   on ☐   sun ☐   up ☐

Word List

Words in pink appear only in the art on the Conversation Time pages.

A

a	page 3
actor	49
ah-choo	5
am	27
an	19
angry	25
animal	47
Annie	2
ant	40
apples	38
are	1

B

baby	1
bad	41
bag	40
baker	49
ball	4
bananas	38
basketball	54
be quiet	9
beautiful	41
bed	44
bee	15
big	41
bike	54
bird	4
bless you	5
book	18
book bag	17
borrow	37
boy	2
branch	63
bugs	15
burgers	34
bus	60
bush	5
butterfly	6
bye-bye	57

C

can	55
can't	55
car	54
carrots	38
cartwheel	58
cat	10
caterpillar	15
chicken	10
close	vii
cloud	6
circle	vii
climb a tree	54
cold	26
cow	10
cow pasture	47
crayon	17
cucumbers	38

D

dad	53
dance	57
desk	20
dig	52
Digger	2
do	39
do a cartwheel	58
doctor	50
dog	2
don't	35
draw a picture	54
drive a car	54
duck	20

E

egg	44
eight	22
eleven	22
equals	31
eraser	18

F

fat	42
feel	41
feet	28
fifteen	21
fine	1
finished	33
firefighter	50
first	21
fish	28
five	22
flower	6
fly	15
fly a kite	58
fork	28
four	22
fourteen	21
friend	53
frog	5

G

garden	8
girl	2
goat	10
going	57
good morning	1
gorilla	8
grapes	37
guitar	58

H

hand	24
happy	26
hat	40
he	43
hello	1
here you are	17
he's	43
hi	1
hot	26

hot dogs	33
horse	10
house	24
how are you	1
hungry	26
hurry	33

I

I think so	25
I'm	3
in	52
is	7
isn't	19
it	19
it's	11

J

jump	57
jump rope	53

K

kangaroo	8
key	8
kite	8

L

lake	6
last	21
leaf	63
like	35
line	vii
listen	vi

M

mail carrier	50
make a circle	vii
make a line	vii
make a sandwich	58
man	1